THE VINE AND THE BRANCHES

WITHDRAWN

Eight Sermons For The Easter Season

BY JERRY L. SCHMALENBERGER

C.S.S Publishing Co., Inc.
Lima, Ohio

Copyright © 1992 by
The C.S.S. Publishing Company, Inc.
Lima, Ohio

This is a revised edition of "Resurrection: Checking The Vital Signs," Sermons For The Easter Season, copyrighted 1981 by C.S.S. Publishing Co., and originally numbered C.S.S. 1808, ISBN 0-89536-501-4.

Library of Congress Cataloging-in-Publication Data

Schmalenberger, Jerry L.
    The vine and the branches : sermons for the Easter season / by Jerry L. Schmalenberger.
        p.   cm.
    Rev. ed. of: Resurrection. 1981
    ISBN 1-55673-403-4
    1. Eastertide—Sermons.   2. Sermons, American,
I. Schmalenberger, Jerry L. Resurrection.   II. Title.
    BV4259.S36   1992
252'.63—dc20   91-31289
                                                      CIP

9216 / ISBN 1-55673-403-4   PRINTED IN U.S.A.

I am the vine, you are the branches. Those who abide in me and I in them bear much fruit, because apart from me you can do nothing.

John 15:5

Acknowledgements

Material from *Braude's Handbook of Humor for All Occasions* by Jacob M. Braude, copyright 1958 by Prentice Hall, Inc. and published by Prentice-Hall, Inc., Englewood Cliffs, New Jersey, appears on the following pages: Joke #1345 on page 17, Joke #321 on page 30, Joke #48 on page 26, and Joke #299 on page 59.

Scripture quotations are from the New Revised Standard Version of the Bible, copyright 1989 by the Division of Christian Education of the National Council of the Churches of Christ in the USA. Used by permission.

Table of Contents

Don't Be Alarmed

In the *Des Moines Register* was a story titled, "Man, Believed Killed by Log, Sits on It." "It happened in Hamburg, Wisconsin. William Bartelt, 71, of Hamburg, was recovering in a Wausau hospital Saturday after friends gave him up for dead after a log struck him on the head. Bartelt was hit by a limb cut down by his hired hand at his central Wisconsin farm, officials said. The limb knocked him out and the hired hand, Gerhardt Stueber, determined that Bartelt was not breathing and called relatives to the scene, authorities said. Coroner Marv Nelles was alerted, and a funeral home dispatched a vehicle to recover the body. Nelles found the elderly man sitting on the log that struck him, sheriff's officers said."

I bet that was a jolt for good old Nelles who had called the funeral home. Can't you see the face of the funeral director as he pulled up the coach and found the deceased sitting on that log?

We don't know what Nelles and the other farmers said or even what the deceased man come back to life said. We do know what a young man said when they came for the same purpose to claim Jesus' body: "Don't be alarmed!" Wow! Bad enough that William Bartelt of Hamburg got knocked out by a log, and then they found him alive! Imagine those women who saw Jesus killed on a cross and buried in a tomb with a rock in the door. Now the tomb was empty and he was gone.

There had not been time to render the last service to the body of Jesus. The Sabbath had intervened and the women who wished to anoint the body had not been able to do so. Now the Sabbath had passed and, as early as possible, they set out on their sad task. They were worried about one thing: how to get the large round stone rolled away so that they could get into the rock cave. But, when they reached the tomb, the stone was rolled away, and in it there was a messenger who gave them the unbelievable news that Jesus had risen from the dead!

"As they entered the tomb, they saw a young man, dressed in a white robe, sitting on the right side; and they were alarmed. But he said to them, "Do not be alarmed; you are looking for Jesus of Nazareth who was crucified. He has been raised; he is not here. Look, this is the place they laid him (Mark 16:5, 6a)."

One thing is certain. If Jesus had not risen from the dead, we would never have heard of him!

The attitude of the women was that they had come to pay their last tribute to a dead body. The attitude of the disciples was that everything had finished in tragedy. (Sometimes it appears that way.)

By far, the best proof of the resurrection is the existence of the Christian Church. Nothing else could have changed sad and despairing men and women into people radiant with joy and flaming with courage. I'll bet you've seen, as I've seen, the same thing at the funeral home, in the hospital corridor, at the courtroom. The resurrection is a central fact of the whole Christian faith. It is the great amen for us. It is the vital sign that God was in Jesus Christ and is with us now.

One of Ernest Poole's characters in one of his poetic novels says: "History is just news from the graveyard." Well, I'll agree that all of history is shaped by the news from one graveyard, a garden outside Jerusalem, about the year A.D. 30. The best news of all the world and of all the years is from that graveyard outside of Jerusalem with a tomb that was empty, and one who had laid there standing before all humanity for all time with the assurance: "I am the resurrection and the life. Those who believe in me, even though they die, will live, and everyone who lives and believes in me will never die (John 11:25-26)."

Easter is the good news about the universe and about Almighty God and about myself. It proclaims that the world is not some kind of an orphan asylum. It is not a mammoth machine shop. It is not a whirling ball hurtling through endless space. It is a home, and its heart is not something the scientists are always looking for — the source of life — the heart of it is someone. It is the breathtaking news that the risen and living Lord is here and alive.

Here are our life and faith as his disciples. We don't gather today to gaze into an empty tomb. We don't pass by a casket to view the remains. Rather, we gather to hear again that messenger say to our lives — don't be alarmed; he is risen. He has risen — not to heaven but to be with us. Some things can scare the pants off of you. Nuclear fallout, weapons, wars, inflation, depression, running out of energy, can all be very terrifying in our day. That's why we need not to live lives of alarm but, rather, peace.

Don't be alarmed. You now see that he is alive today. Don't let the death of a loved one alarm you. Don't let illness and threats of your own death scare you. Don't allow alarm about being alone here. Don't let guilt you know haunt your life. Don't be afraid — remove the fear. Because he is risen, God has won — he is with us here and we need not be alarmed. We are not a cult of people remembering a dead martyr. For that reason, I'm always a little uneasy about all the lilies around the chancel area at Easter time. Our leader is not dead; this is not a funeral; we are not here to grieve or mourn. We are a group of disciples celebrating his life with us in this place and throughout all of our daily routine.

At an Easter Family Service when I asked the kids what happened to Jesus that we celebrate on that day, one little boy popped up loudly enough for the entire congregation to hear: "He *riz!*" I am surely certain that that was more acceptable to God than the response of the disciples when the women told them that they had found the tomb empty. They called it, properly translated, gibberish.

When a doctor wants to know the condition of a patient, he asks for the vital signs. Pulse, heartbeat, respiration, and the patient's response to stimuli are recorded. We are that once dead body now alive. It looked as though Jesus, God's Son, was killed forever on Good Friday. But now we know differently. He is alive today — we have moved from dark Lent to a bright and alive Easter.

Back then, the body came to life after the ugly of the day had murdered it. It came alive and walked out of the tomb in which it had been placed.

Today, the body comes alive again. The vital signs prove its life: there is a heart beating here for all who need its love and comfort. There is breath here for all who thirst for something more significant in their lives. There is a response here to those who have needs the body can supply. There is a response here that says this body is no longer dead and stiff but, rather, alive and vital.

We are not alarmed about what those soldiers did on Calvary. Instead, we are jubilant today that he lived again back then and he lives again in and through us.

That's why you look different today. That's why there is a radiance in your faces and a ring of joy in your voices. It's more than the good music and large attendance, too. It's more than spring's arrival. He is risen, he is alive in us and all the vital signs are here to prove it. No longer need we be alarmed.

Because we believe in the resurrection, certain things follow. They are the vital signs of his aliveness now in our congregation and in our lives.

Jesus is not a figure in a book; he is a living presence. It's not enough to study the story of Jesus as we study the life of any other great historical figure. It may be that we begin that way, but we must end by meeting him. Jesus is not a memory; he is a presence. The Greeks had a word by which they described time which means: "time which wipes all things out."

Long since, time would have wiped out the meaning of Jesus unless he had been a living presence forever with us. That means that the Christian life is not the life of a person who knows about Jesus, but of the person who knows Jesus. We know about Winston Churchill and about the Ayotollah Khomeini and about President Reagan, but we don't know them.

Isaiah says, "Lo, this is our God; we have waited for him, so that he might save us. This is the Lord for whom we have waited; let us be glad and rejoice in his salvation (Isaiah 25:9)."

Probably the greatest tragedy of the first Easter day was the fact that everyone to whom our Lord had given reason for waiting and trusting in him had forgotten his words. And now, on Easter day, we have the assurance that it is as he said on that day.

A time-study expert indicates that if a man lives with the same woman for 50 years, he will spend at least a month and a half of that 50 years just waiting for her someplace, whether it's for her to get her makeup on, or to find her purse, or whatever. The expert didn't say anything about how long a wife would have to wait for a husband while she's keeping dinner warm and he's late from work. Or how long we have to wait for one of our teenagers to get off the telephone. That's another story. No human being can escape it. It's part and parcel of our human experience to be waiting and hoping. The Jews were waiting since Isaiah and now no longer — he is here.

Today he comes out of the grave to be alive and with us here. We can take him by the hand and he'll go home with us. And when we grieve and when we celebrate and rejoice, he is with us.

There is a story of two garment workers in New York City. One was a cutter and one was a stitcher. They were working side by side. They got to talking about vacations. One said he was looking forward to his vacation and the other said he was not going on a vacation this year. The question was asked, "Why?" "I went to Africa last year. I went elephant hunting." "Did you get any elephants?" "No, I found an elephant. He charged me, but my gun was jammed, and I was killed." "What are you talking about, you was killed? You aren't dead. You're sitting here living." And the other replied: "You call this living?" And that's what many of us ask. Do you call this living? Easter sounds a resounding yes. Here is resurrection and the life. As his family — as the saved, as the people who gather here and worship him. This is indeed living! We are the resurrection people and we live on this side of Easter.

When we baptize and commune, when we gather for worship and study, he is alive in us and with us. We become the full person he intends us to be. So no longer need we be alarmed.

The most precious thing in this passage is in two words which are in no other gospel: "Go" said the messenger, "give the message to his disciples, *including* Peter (v. 7)."

How that message must have cheered Peter's heart when he got it! He must have been tortured with the memory of his disloyalty, and suddenly there comes a message, a special message for *him*! He, of all the disciples, is specifically picked out. It is characteristic of Jesus that he thought, not at all of the wrong Peter had done him, but altogether of the remorse that Peter was undergoing. Take heart in that! Jesus was far more eager to comfort the penitential sinner than to punish the sin. Think what that means to us as his family. We need not be alarmed about our past. Rather, Jesus as an alive presence assures us of his complete forgiveness and his desire that we start again with him today. Go — tell the disciples, *including* Peter — and including us.

James Russell Lowell said: "I take great comfort in God. I think he is considerably amused at us many times, but he loves us, and he would not let us get at the matchbox as carelessly as he does, unless he knew the framework of his universe is fireproof."

Easter means . . . the vindication, the triumph, of Jesus and all he stands for. Easter invites us to forget ourselves and all of our worries or doubts or speculations over personal survival, and to think of him. If Jesus, and what he stands for, is the thing that must survive and triumph; if your world is to be rational and your life to be livable in it — then you already have the beginning of a faith in the resurrection, and the most important element in that faith. For, from first to last, the New Testament faith is an assurance, a conviction of the ultimate triumph, not merely of us, in our own tiny private lives, but of God himself and of Christ and all that Christ stands for in this world.

14

I know that my Redeemer lives!
What comfort this sweet sentence gives!
He lives, he lives, who once was dead;
He lives, my everliving head!

He lives to silence all my fears;
He lives to wipe away my tears;
He lives to calm my troubled heart;
He lives all blessings to impart.
                    — Samuel Medley 1738-1799

If this worship experience feels good to you and you're a visitor, be assured this is the way it is with Christians every Sunday and throughout the week. If you've tried it going alone long enough, try it with us and the living presence of Christ. If you will allow Christ to come out of the place you have buried him — he'll be alive with you also.

How nice that he told them to be sure Peter got the message! Here is hope for those who deny or forget or become apathetic; his message is, He is risen and be sure to tell them. Thank God for Peter in this Easter story! If the disciples had been perfect, I couldn't bear it today. But they weren't. God didn't want to punish. He wanted to forgive and to be with even Peter!

When the great battle of Waterloo in 1812 pitted the nations of Europe against the growing might of Napoleon's dictatorship, upon its outcome hung the destiny of millions. With binoculars focused on European soil across the channel waters, anxious watchers awaited the signal flags which would spell out the message of victory or defeat. It was a dark day with mist restricting visibility, but hearts sank as the first words flashed: "Wellington defeated . . ." This was the end, they said, who stood on the white cliffs of Dover. But when the fog lifted it was the final word that brought renewed vision. The full message was "Wellington defeated Napoleon." Until the morning light was breaking, until God opened their blinded eyes to spiritual reality, the sad truth appeared to be "Christ defeated."

Pilate and Annas and Caiaphas could rub their hands in glee and satisfaction and say, "Well, we have heard the last of him. That's the end of the King of the Jews." But when the sun has risen, we know the full truth. "Christ defeated his enemies. Christ defeated sin. Christ defeated death itself."

Good news for bad times we have here:

> *Be not alarmed,*
> *As we bury and wonder.*
> *As the world seems out of control,*
> *As we seem to be defeated,*
> *As we diminish our natural resources.*

Don't be alarmed — God is still in control and is with us.

"Don't be alarmed," he said, "I know you are looking for Jesus of Nazareth, who was crucified. He is not here — he has been raised." Amen.

When Thomas Doubted

A German was the guest of a Frenchman who asked him how they distinguished between an optimist and a pessimist in Germany. "It is very simple," replied the German. "The optimists are learning English and the pessimists are learning Russian!" Thomas would be learning Russian! One person has described a pessimist as someone who burns his bridges behind him and then crosses them before he gets to them. Another claims a pessimist is one who, of two evils, chooses them both! That may well describe Thomas.

To Thomas, the cross was only what he had expected. When Jesus had suggested going to Bethany, when the news of the illness of Lazarus had come, Thomas' reaction had been: "Let us also go, that we may die with him (John 11:16)."

Thomas never lacked courage, but Thomas was a natural pessimist. What Thomas had expected to happen had happened. When it came, Thomas was broken-hearted. So broken-hearted was he that he wanted to be alone with his grief. John picks up the story: "One of the twelve disciples, Thomas (called the twin), was not with them when Jesus came. So the other disciples told him, 'We have seen the Lord!' Thomas said to them, 'Unless I see the scars of the nails in his hands and put my finger on those scars and my hand in his side, I will not believe."

So it happened that, when Jesus came back again, Thomas was not there. The news that Jesus had risen seemed to him far too good to be true, and he refused to believe it.

Thomas not appearing with the disciples on that first Sunday after Easter may have furnished a measure of the depth of his sorrow and disappointment. At the death of his child, one of England's poets cried out, "Never will I risk such

17

anguish again. I will never love anything anymore." Thomas felt that way, too!

So another week elapsed and Jesus came back again; and this time Thomas was there. And Jesus knew Thomas' heart. He repeated Thomas' own words and invited Thomas to make the test that he had demanded.

"Then he said to Thomas, 'Put your finger here and see my hands. Reach out your hand and put it in my side. Do not doubt but believe.' Thomas answered him, 'My Lord and my God (vv. 27, 28)!''

In this story, the chapter of Thomas stands out clear before us. He made a serious mistake. He withdrew from Christian fellowship. He sought loneliness rather than togetherness. In the second chapter of Acts, we read how Christians are described. "They devoted themselves to the apostles' teaching and fellowship, to the breaking of bread and the prayers . . . All who believed were together and had all things in common . . . (Acts 2:42, 44a)." Because he was not there with his fellow Christians, he missed the first coming of Jesus.

We miss so very much when we separate ourselves from the Christian fellowship and when we try to go it alone. Things can happen to us here that can't when we are alone. When sorrow and grief come to us, we often tend to shut ourselves up and to refuse to meet people. That is the time, in spite of our sorrow, when we should seek the fellowship of Christ's people. It is there we are most likely to meet him face-to-face.

Our loyalty needs to go way beyond a pastor, choir director, church secretary, etc. This story of Thomas and his behavior is right on target for us now. If Jesus died on the cross and is now just a dead martyr, we can remember him with flowers on the altar and let it go at that. We can, then, dissipate our energies in choosing up sides over silly incidentals in the congregation like what hymns we sing, how we usher, how the parking lot is managed, and what the preacher's kids wear to church.

But, if Christ came out of the tomb on Easter and is alive here, these considerations become so trivial compared to how we will see him alive in our church and who needs him most and how best can we love him in our getting together as a congregation. Christ alive makes us the resurrection people.

Thomas got side-tracked for a while. He left the other believers just when he needed them the most. So, he found himself mourning over a dead Jesus instead of being with a live Christ. This led him to be concerned with trivia, like his own ego and the size of the holes in Jesus' hands and side.

Come on, Thomas, get off incidentals and get with the live God at your side.

We don't know, either, what the other disciples were doing about Thomas' absence. We hope they were concerned and perhaps had even delegated one of their group to seek him out and plead for his return.

It is a vital sign of the Christ of Easter now alive. His people get together. That being together calms fears and rids us of our misgivings. Like Thomas, we often separate ourselves from the fellowship of believers just when we most need it. What pastor hasn't heard the heart-breaking comment of a member ashamed of his/her behavior: "I'll never be able to go back to church again."

Yet, that is precisely why the Christ had to come alive and come back to be with us. God well knows we'll doubt; we will fall off the wagon; we sin over and over again. So the assembled believers, the called out of the world by God, become his life presence here in this town, in this neighborhood, where we can have again his forgiving love and his warmth and assurance.

How many times the story could be told. Some little thing like not liking the preacher's spouse or the way the bulletin is printed or we don't get our way in a meeting — so we leave. However, that is the time we most need to be with the rest of the believers, so that we might work it through. So we might put earthly things in our lives into a proper perspective.

A person loses a child and so leaves the church;
Another finds out something about the pastor and leaves;
Still another goes to college and has those lovely Bible
stories blasted to bits.

19

That's no time to leave. Together we, whom God loves and saves, need to be here with the rest over and over again. It's a vital element to our spiritual lives. It's a vital sign to the rest of the community.

One of the legends which grew up about Thomas relates that some years after the event, Thomas was again plagued with doubts about the resurrection. He sought some of the Apostles and began to pour out his soul's troubles to them. But after a while, one by one, the apostles left him because of pressing duties. He made his way to some loyal women in the company of believers. They were surprised at his questions, but like Dorcas, they were busy in labors for the Master and let him know they didn't have time for such thoughts as these. At last, it dawned on Thomas that it was because they were so occupied in the work of the Lord that they were free from the doubt that seemed to be torturing him. He took the hint. He went to Parthia and flung himself into preaching the Word and ministering to the needs of the saints, and was never again troubled with doubt.

"Thomas had two great virtues. He refused to say he believed when he did not. There is an uncompromising honesty about Thomas. He would never still his doubts by pretending they did not exist. He wouldn't rattle off a Creed without understanding what it was all about. Thomas had to be sure. There is more ultimate faith in the person who insists on being sure than in the person who glibly repeats things which he/she has never thought out and which he/she does not really believe. It is doubt like that which ends in certainty."[1]

The Interpreter's Bible has said: " 'What this parish needs,' wrote Carlyle, 'is what every parish needs, a man who knows God at more than second-hand.' Only when the gospel of Christ is for us no carried story, no rumor heard and passed on by us for what it may be worth; but firsthand evidence, what we have seen, what we have looked upon with our own eyes, what we have handled with our own hands, what we have proved in our own experience, not simply an unthinking acquiescence in what others say, which may be all very well as a beginning, but something that has happened to *us* — only then does our belief grow vital. Yet Christ tells us here that there is a bigger faith even than that, a faith that can dispense with tangible proofs and visible evidence, that believes heroically even when there is no obvious and immediate confirmation, building unafraid and confident on God's naked word."[2]

It's something to have the witness of a person like that, that Jesus was alive! No fly-by-night person, one who had to see for himself.

"Thomas' other great virtue was that when he was sure, he went the whole way.' Thomas answered him, "My Lord and My God (v. 28).' " There were no halfway measures about Thomas." He wasn't airing his doubts in order to get out of pledging or serving or giving. "He doubted in order to be sure and when he became sure, his surrender to certainty was complete. If we fight our way through our doubts to the conviction that Jesus Christ is Lord, we then attain a certainty that those who unthinkingly accept things can never reach."[3]

It is this half-hearted surrender with reservation, cautious commitment, that works against our ever knowing him alive with us here. So often we try to live our Christian lives straddling the fence, mouthing the liturgies and creeds and worship of God; but still living our lives by the world's standards and priorities. It's a miserable way to live. We know real stewardship is to at least tithe our income to an alive Christ. Still, we tip him like a gift of memorial to a dead God. We know our lives are enriched when we share Christ with other people. However, we don't. We are like rivers running into the North Sea — all frozen up at the mouth! We know we should love our enemies; but we barely do that for our friends and so never know the cleansing effect that can have on our lives.

We heard all our life that we have complete forgiveness of our guilt here, but we rarely take that seriously. So, we don't enjoy that "freeing up" to be the whole person God intended us to be — ever.

We could go on and on:

The pure in heart are blessed.
The peace-makers are happy.
The meek will inherit.

But we don't try for a completely pure heart, or a peace-maker, or a meek spirit. So we limp along like Thomas did for a while, never knowing for sure or realizing fully the alive God with us.

Paul said about some of his members that "they were neither hot nor cold" and that made him want to throw up!

When we can throw ourselves wholeheartedly into being a part of the live body, we no longer have to doubt nor do others who see us. For in us, then, they see one of the vital signs of a live Christ out of the grave and with us.

"When they began to fling that suspension bridge across the Niagara Gorge, it all began with engineers flying a kite across the chasm, playing out the kite string until the kite reached the farther store. Then twine was tied to the string, and rope to the twine, and wire to the rope, and cable to the wire. In due time, mighty cables were suspended from great towers and anchored on either side in the depths of the earth, and the bridge was built."[4]

John Rilling says: "So the apostolic faith, erected by the hand of God, carries you and me and generations through time to the further stores. But it all began with the frail strands of men like Peter, Paul, James and John and Thomas — doubting Thomas. What the Lord did for them he can do through them for us, if we only let him."[5]

Faith of our fathers, living still
In spite of dungeon, fire, and sword.
Oh, how our hearts beat high with joy.
When-e'er we hear that glorious word.
Faith of our fathers, holy Faith,
We will be true to thee till death.
— Frederick W. Faber, 1814-1863

22

Maybe Thomas has been maligned! Once he did voice his doubts and honestly worked through them, he went all out in his devotion and service.

I think I would be willing to have a congregation full of Thomases. Think what it would mean if we could get off dead center and commit ourselves fully to the alive Christ here:

If we all tithed, we'd triple the income and could support missions and ministry all over the world.

If we all witnessed to our faith, we'd grow by leaps and bounds. Hundreds would join at this altar every few weeks for baptisms and confirmations.

If we all loved and forgave and served others like we should as his disciples, we'd set this community on its ear.

Sunday school would not be able to hold all the adult students studying the Bible! We'd have to add twice the number of worship services to hold all the people! The choir loft would be bulging and you could hear the hymn singing all the way up Sixth Avenue! Musicals would take place. People would be talking about it all over town. It would be a mighty powerful vital sign!

No one was ever less of a stained-glass saint than Thomas. It was always Thomas' first reaction not to do what he was told to do, and not to believe what he was asked to believe. The task offered to him was always too tough for him to attempt, and the good news too good to be true. But the fact he believed with some difficulty made him believe with a fierce intensity once he was convinced. And it was never an argument which solved Thomas' doubts; it was always the presence of his Lord. He again and again made the discovery that every Christian has to make — that by himself/herself everything is possible, but with God, nothing is impossible.

Let's learn from Thomas:

Give ourselves completely to the Lord.
Admit our doubts and work through them.
Keep in the company of the rest of the believers.

"We do not know for sure what happened to Thomas in afterdays — there is an Apocrypha book called the Acts of Thomas which gives us some history.

After the Ascension of Jesus, the disciples divided up the world, so each might go to some country to preach the gospel. India fell by lot to Thomas. The Christians of India do trace their heritage to Thomas."[6]

"Faith was never an easy thing for Thomas; obedience never came readily to him. He had to be sure. He had to count the cost. But once he was sure and had counted the cost, Thomas was the person who went to the ultimate limits of faith and obedience."[7] And so can we! Amen.

Easter 3
Luke 24:36-49

Checking The Vital Signs

It was Easter Sunday. One thousand, seven hundred fifty showed up for worship that day. Boy, was this place full! And it really felt good. We sang some of the same hymns as today. I gave the kids red Easter eggs and my sermon title was: "Don't Be Alarmed." The main idea was that Christ is alive and with us, so there need not be any event or situation in our lives here that should scare us. In addition, even at our death and the death of the people we love, we need not have any fear since Christ has come out of the grave and has arranged for us to do the same!

Today, two weeks later, I want to consider what difference it has made in our lives that Easter happened again this year. I want you to think over, with me, the last two weeks and consider just how alive he has been with you.

The gospel for the day records: They were startled and terrified, and thought that they were seeing a ghost. He said to them, "Why are you frightened, and why do doubts arise in your hearts? Look at my hands and my feet; see that it is I myself. Touch me and see; for a ghost does not have flesh and bones as you see that I have (vv. 37-39)."

Probably today our Lord would say: "Check my vital signs and you can see that I'm alive." There are different ways you can test out whether a person is really alive. The medical profession tells me that the vital signs are respiration, pulse and heartbeat, temperature, and something they call response.

There are different ways you can test out whether Christ really did come out of the tomb two weeks ago and has changed your life as well. Whether we still worship a dead martyr or a living presence is crucial to our faith, to the life of this congregation, and to the people who know us. Just like we have vital signs that tell whether our body is alive, we also have vital signs that we can check to see if the Body of Christ, this congregation and we, as individual Christians, are alive.

A woman devoted to Christ once adopted a peculiar method of shaming her Christian friends. She was found testifying to her faith before a wooden Indian in front of a cigar store. She was chided for the scene she created and then defended herself by saying: "I would rather be a real Christian and talk religion to a wooden Indian than a wooden Christian who never talked religion to anyone!"

Perhaps the best vital sign of all is whether anyone has noticed the difference since Easter. One of the vital signs that is checked to see if a person is alive is called respiration. That is, we check to see if breath is going in and out of the body.

When Jesus came out of the grave that first Easter and then became an alive presence with his disciples, it made them different people. Some accused them of being drunk; later many were nicknamed "Fools for Christ." Others said they were crazy. They were so excited about his not being killed forever that they just had to share that risen Savior.

Verse 48 of the gospel for the day says: "You are witnesses of these things. And so when additional disciples were selected, they were always selected to be "witnesses to the resurrection."

Has your life changed any in the last couple weeks since Easter and the resurrection? After all, the Christian faith is a lot like the measles — you catch it — It's a holy infection!

A stranger came into a doctor's office and said, "I just dropped in to tell you how much I benefited from your treatment." The doctor replied, "But you are not one of my patients." "I know," the stranger replied, "but my uncle was and I'm his heir."

Sometimes our witness is so dull. We seem like a dead corpse instead of a living presence.

If Christ is alive and with you, he'll be noticed. He'll be obvious to other people who see the way you make up your priorities and live out your Christian faith. I suppose we could say the respiration hasn't been quite as exhilarating or as obvious as it was on Easter morning for the Body of Christ, called this congregation. About half of the people who were there that day are here today. One little committee went out and made some evangelism calls since that time. Some shared about a percent and a half of their income in the offering. A small group sang in the choir the second Sunday of Easter.

Do you really think that's vitally alive? Do you think people who have never been here before, worshiping with us for the first time today, can see a vital sign of our lives being changed and our worship being enthusiastic and so the respiration of this body giving a positive, alive, vital sign? Let's remember Easter morning and all that means to how we ought to be since that day.

> *Breathe on me breath of God, Fill me with life anew,*
> *That I may love all that you love, And do what you*
> *would do.*
> *Breathe on me, breath of God, Until my heart is pure,*
> *Until with you I will one will To do and to endure.*
> *— Edwin Harch 1835-1889 (From LBW-1978)*

Another vital sign is the heartbeat or pulse. This has to do with the blood racing through the body. One of othe signs of the "live Christ" with the disciples was in the way they got together and communed. It began as a celebration of his real presence. He was known to them by the way he broke bread.

We offered that same bread and wine on a Sunday of Easter, and he was here with us. Seven hundred and sixty of the 1,700 present took of that sacrament. That's 46 percent of the body that decided to be here when he had promised to be with us in a special way.

Do you think 46 percent heartbeat or pulse rate is about right? Do you think that is an accurate reflection of how alive the Body of Christ is here?

Easter came on the first day of the week, and ever since that great event his followers have gathered on Sunday to worship him and to be with him. Remember Easter? Check it out this way — how often have you been at worship since that day of lilies, Easter eggs and fine clothing?

The risen Christ, if he is alive and with you, will certainly make you want to be with his people and a part of that pulse and heartbeat which says that he is alive here.

Last week we saw the danger of doubts and disbelief Thomas ran into when he was not with the other believers. It sounds to me like we should sing, "He is risen and out of my hair," rather than, "He is risen and with me now. Alleluia."

Bruce Baxter tells of an unusual custom which is observed in a small English chapel at evening service. "At the end of each pew is a tall candlestick. When the family that customarily uses that pew is ushered in, the candle is lighted. When the family is not present, the pew remains dark. Obviously, the amount of light in the chapel is determined by the number of families present that evening."

Whether or not we come to worship is more than a decision about our busyness at home or desire to do other things. We are a part of the pulse of the Body of Christ and one of the vital signs that communicates to the rest of the people around us whether Christ is really out of the grave and alive again.

Jesus gave us another test. He said, according to John's gospel, "Those who love me will keep my word, and my Father will love them, and we will come to them and make our home with them (John 14:23)."

In other words, if he is really alive and with us, we will obey his commands — his rules of conduct for us.

One of those commands was very specific. Jesus told his disciples that when someone was hungry or thirsty or cold and we gave help, we were actually ministering to him. So being an alive Christ means being very concerned about people — whether they are a prisoner, an alcoholic, someone suffering injustice because of color or age or creed or sex or political beliefs. In the Scripture today our Lord asks, in verse 42, to receive a piece of cooked fish, and he ate it in their presence. He later claimed that when we fed someone who was hungry, we were actually doing the same as those disciples were when they gave him that fish.

28

When John the Baptist's disciples went to Jesus to see if he was real, Jesus told them, "Go back home and tell John what you see." What they saw was that the blind were healed and the lame walked. People are helped in whatever situation they are in; this is called Social Ministry in our congregation. It's really God's hands in the community; it's the risen Easter Christ alive through this congregation of believers. It's one of the great vital signs of the church. When people are fed, clothed, comforted, and have their dignity restored, the vital sign says that Christ is indeed alive here.

If we have ignored the appeals for world hunger and for justice, if our congregation is not moved by the poor who live in our community and those who have no power in our society, the vital sign is not there. That means that Christ did not come out of the grave for us and he is still in the tomb, and we gather this day to put flowers around that tomb and simply sing sentimental hymns to his memory.

Reliable reports state that up to 500 million people are suffering extreme hunger in our world. According to United Nations' statistics, "The single most devastating indictment of our current world civilization is the continued existence of stark, pervasive poverty of more than two-thirds of the world's population." If Christ is really alive, then we're pouring out our resources to try to help this situation. It's certainly one of the vital signs.

The medical people have another vital sign which they call response. It checks out with persons how they respond to stimuli, whether they can talk to us and answer questions, whether they say "ouch" when we pinch them, and just how much they respond to what they see and hear around them.

Certainly this also would be a vital sign that we could use to test if Jesus really came back from the dead on Easter morning and lives with us now, or if he is still in that grave.

One of the ways that we can test if he is alive, and if we are properly responding, would be with where we spend our money. Our Lord told us that to have him with us meant a new set of priorities. He told us in Matthew 6 not to save treasures for ourselves here on earth where thieves can break in and steal. He alerted us to the fact that our heart will always be where our riches are. So, if Jesus is really alive with us, our offerings will have said so by now. If we're still giving the one dollar per Sunday that we gave 10 or 20 years ago, Christ did not come out of that grave. He's still in there deteriorating.

The doctor was taken to the patient's room but came down in a few minutes and asked for a screwdriver. Five minutes later he was back and asked for a can opener. Soon after he returned and demanded a chisel and hammer. The distraught husband could not stand it any longer. "Please, Doc, what's wrong with my wife?" "Don't know yet," the doc answered. "Can't get my bag open."

Response is to open our bags and billfolds and respond to the needs of people all around us.

I believe that the practice of serious stewardship is a direct vital sign on the liveness of Christ in any congregation of believers. In fact, sometimes it appears as though we have a dead Savior on our hands, or at least one who is in a coma and getting weaker and weaker each Sunday that we come together.

After all, we live in a society where cash is very important to us. Is Christ alive in us if we spend three to five dollars to see a movie and give 50 cents a week in the offering? I do know that if we tell our spouses that we love them very dearly and then are terribly stingy with them, they know that something is wrong and we really aren't being truthful.

Some could say that this vital sign should never be mentioned in the pulpit. Yet, two-thirds of our Lord's parables have dealt with this very subject. I'm not just making a plea for your money today; I'm making a plea for Christianity to be practiced. For the vital sign of response to be real in this congregation, Christianity is not just alive in our checkbooks like we said he would be on Easter morning! Our offerings are more like buying a spray of flowers for the casket at the graveside rather than supporting a live and vital God in our midst.

A. J. Gossip said: "You will not stroll into Christ-likeness with your hands in your pockets, shoving open the door with a careless shoulder. This is not a hobby for one's leisure moments, taken up at intervals when we have nothing much to do, and put down and forgotten when our life grows full and interesting."

Very often in our Sunday to Sunday lives we are guilty of living by a comparative religion. Our giving and our doing "for Christ" are very carefully measured by what others around us are doing. Instead, we need to realize that our trusteeship of life is a gift from God. As trustees, we have opportunity to use all he has given us in a faithful way as if he is really alive and with us here.

Do you, when you give your offering, sense the living Christ within you? Does your offering say that he came out of the grave or that he's still buried? It is one of the vital signs.

Of course, response of an alive body here is more than money. But we Americans understand money. It's our language, our way of life, so it's definitely a vital sign called response. Response of the live body is also how we respond to all God has given us, how we respond to the sacraments, the means of grace. When we are asked to serve in a special way, when Sunday school teachers are needed, people to help with vacation church school, youth sponsors, volunteers to call and pledge — the test is continually applied to the body to see if it is alive and real or dead and beginning to get stiff!"

One other test — have your words been kind? In a time when criticism is so easy and judgment so prevalent, we need to remember that tender attitude of our risen Christ. ". . . and in his name the message about repentance and the forgiveness of sins must be preached to all nations, beginning in Jerusalem." Remember our Lord said, ". . . be kind to each other?" Have you done that? Remember Easter? The God that couldn't stay killed on Calvary was a God of love. That love ought to radiate from us as a congregation and as an individual these two weeks that we call Easter weeks. It was said of Henry Ward Beecher that no one ever felt the full force of his kindness until he/she did Beecher an injury.

Life is most froth and bubbles,
only two things stand like stone,
kindness and another's troubles,
courage and your own.

When Eugene Debs was imprisoned as a conscientious objector, he became interested in a black prisoner who was said to be incorrigible, devoid of a spark of goodness. Since the black person would not speak to anyone, Debs started a campaign of kindness by leaving an orange on the black's bed and going off without a word. In spite of many rebuffs, he gradually penetrated the hard exterior of the man, and the two became fast friends. Years later, at the news of Debs' death, the black person, now a useful citizen, made this comment: "He was the only Jesus Christ I ever knew."

If we continue to gossip, to judge, and to slander, to put the worst construction on our fellow person's actions. Christ is not alive in us. He has been killed again and we have need of yet another Easter and another resurrection.

Congregations can be mean. Christians can be mean. The way we present the good news can be all law and terribly demanding. If someone is checking the vital signs of the risen Christ and sees this kind of attitude, that person will be sure he is dead and never came out of that grave.

Love is a beautiful thing. The God of Easter is a God of love and he wants one of the signs of the congregation to be an accepting and beautiful love that is not sentimental but is carried out in actions and justice.

When I came home after preaching to those 1,700 people, I promised myself that in two weeks I would revisit that "Easter high" and test out if it was really true that you and I had experienced again God coming out of the grave so that he might be with us. Today we have applied the medical vital signs to test if that body is alive. We have checked the pulse, checked the respiration, looked at the temperature, and watched for response. You decide. Is he alive and with us, or have we just gathered to remember again his burial?

"You are witnesses of these things." Amen.

One Flock, One Shepherd

One of the vital signs of an alive Christ with us here is whether this live body out of the grave is seeking unity, oneness with other members and other denominations and other families of God.

Because our Lord prayed for it, because it was so evident during his earthly ministry, and because it is the very heart of the gospel, we know a vital sign of an alive Christ is an aggressive seeking after unity. It is the very nature of an alive group of his disciples.

Let's check the vital sign in our own church.

We quote it when we install a pastor: ". . . I have other sheep that do not belong to this fold. I must bring them also, and they will listen to my voice. So there will be one flock, one shepherd (v. 16)."

It's a beautiful sight — the shepherd gathering his sheep into the sheepfold. In the Middle East, shepherds own a sheepfold in common. It's usually constructed of a stone wall in a circle with brambles on top to keep anything from climbing over. To one side is an opening in the wall where the sheep and goats from several flocks go in and out. Late in the evening, the shepherds will build a fire close to that hole and will lie down right in the hole and use their bodies as a door to the fold. In the morning, you can see those same shepherds riding donkeys out through the fields, playing on their bamboo pipes and sometimes calling out in a beautiful voice, "mena." The sheep know the voice of their shepherd and follow him out to the green pastures for the day.

Jesus tells this story and we use it often to plead for unity in following our pastor — an under-shepherd. We use its rich imagery in talking about the "Good Shepherd." We talk

33

about God as our Shepherd and that we will never have any want as long as the situation is that way.

But shepherds and sheep and folds aren't very much a part of our lives today — only a few of us are farmers; and those use fences instead of shepherds, and barns instead of folds!

Let's concentrate today on that sentence that Jesus adds at the end of this beautiful passage about sheep and shepherds. Because, if we take it seriously, it scolds us and calls us to task for our behavior as one of the sheep in one of the folds of the Good Shepherd.

Jesus says: ". . . And I lay down my life for the sheep. I have other sheep that do not belong to this fold. I must bring them also, and they will listen to my voice. So there will be one flock, one shepherd (v. 15, 16)."

Notice Jesus says one shepherd and one flock, but not one fold. One of the hardest things in the world to unlearn is exclusiveness. Once a people or a group of people get the idea that they are different from other people, it is very difficult for them to realize that the privileges which they believe belong just to them are, in fact, open to all people.

When I was director of a Lutheran church camp in Ohio, I used to read the campers' postcards on the way up the lane to the mailbox. They gave me a good idea of how camp was going that week. One postcard read: "This is the place where the Indian braves threw their old fathers — wish you were here." Another postcard read: "Dear Mom, I changed my underwear today. Having a wonderful time!" But the third postcard was the most interesting. It went like this: "Dear Sis — They make you walk in a pan of chemical water every time before you go in swimming. I think it's so you don't get Catholic's foot."

Paul wrote to his church at Ephesus: "We are no longer strangers . . . Christ has broken down the walls that separate us."

Jesus has said that there is only one shepherd and one flock but many and other folds. Let's say it here, then, that there are many denominations. That is, there are many organizations

34

of Christians. One of them is certainly as legitimate as another. So we have United Methodist, United Presbyterian, Christian, United Church of Christ, Church of God, Nazarene, Lutheran, Pentecostal, and Roman Catholic.

Jesus prayed for his disciples in John 17:18-20a: "As you have sent me into the world, so I have sent them into the world. And for their sakes I sanctify myself, so that they also may be sanctified in truth. . . . That they may all be one."

Yet it is true that five orders of Christians fight over the top of Calvary in Jerusalem to decide who will maintain the building. They fight over which group gets to worship where in the Church of the Holy Sepulchre itself. Our separation in the family of God is a scandal. God intended for us to be friends.

We need to know that genuine disciples of Jesus believe that other denominations are blood brothers and sisters of ours, and belong to the same flock, even when they don't see us in that way.

Just as we show our love in different ways (not all husbands get their wives flowers or all wives send cards with sentimental poetry), down through the years as we have become aware of our God and what he did for us on Calvary, we have worked out different ways to get together and express our thanks.

Lloyd George, the British statesman, once remarked: "The church I belong to is torn in a fierce dispute. One section says that Baptism is *in* the name of the Father, and the other that it is *into* the name of the Father. I belong to one of these parties. I feel most strongly about it. I would die for it, in fact, but I forget which it is."

All religion and worship are a response to a victory already won for us — over ourselves, our sins, our death, over fear and loneliness. One family of God may sing sentimental, experience-centered hymns, which another may use Greek and light candles, and yet another may roll in the aisles and speak in tongues! Still one more denomination may use beautiful classical music and revel in liturgies of ages past. It's not a matter of one being wrong and the other being correct. It's not a matter of one being God's family and all the rest being the devil's. These are God's people celebrating an Easter victory together in the way that best expresses them.

It's a little like it was the day when World War II was over. I remember in the little town of Greenville, Ohio, where I grew up, that some just sat and cried; others shot off fireworks and shotguns into the air; others hugged; and I even remember the firemen drove the fire engine into the park lagoon with the siren still running. All rejoicing about the same thing but in their own way.

Paul puts it in 1 Timothy 2:3-6a: "This is right and is acceptable in the sight of God our Savior, who desires everyone to be saved and to come to the knowledge of the truth. For there is one God; there is also one mediator between God and humankind, Christ Jesus, himself a human, who gave himself a ransom for all — that was attested at the right time."

That's the healthy thing about different churches and denominations — we reach all kinds of God's people. Jesus said it, ". . . one flock and one shepherd . . . and I have others I must lead also." Knowing this to be true, there are some severe warnings for us and our fellow Christians:

1. Don't base your religion on just what you are against. That's Old Testament alone. The "thou shalt nots" belong to the Law and the Old Testament. The New Testament talks more about "blessed are they . . ." and "how much more! . . ." Christians of any denomination are never haters of another. Because of the bitter fight in the church in the 16th century, Protestants sometimes still carry the stigma of being "Catholic haters." How foolish and how shallow that kind of discipleship really is.

Thomas McCaulay, the English historian, returned from the Orient saying: "In a country where people pray to cows, the differences that divide Christians seem of small account." When Isaac Casaubon, the great French scholar, was being shown the Hall of the Sorbonne on the occasion of his first visit to Paris, his guide told him, "This is where the theologians

36

have disputed for 500 years." "Indeed," was the reply, "and pray, what have they settled?"

I find that there is more difference in theological beliefs between members of one congregation because of their refusal to study the Scripture and deepen their spiritual lives than there is between official beliefs of different denominations!

After all, what one of us can claim that we live the life of a disciple so correctly that only *our* religion is correct? If you base your religion only on the negative, that is, what other churches and practices you are against, when you need positive content to get you through, you don't have anything. When you lose a loved one or go through a divorce or get laid off or become lonely, it just doesn't help to be against another denomination.

But what a comfort! What a companionship! What a presence if your fellowship in the family of God has helped you genuinely to know the Good Shepherd.

2. Beware of basing your Christian faith on a person or a church building or a denomination. Buildings can be sold, relocated, burned down, crumble, or fall down. People can build highways through them. Preachers can come and go. They are human and make mistakes. Denominations may merge or go bankrupt. God works through them in different ways. Some are a lot better than others. But so are members!

Don't worship the pastor or the building. Your faith is much bigger than that. In so many instances, those who were the closest friends to the former pastor give the next pastor the most trouble. So beware of getting your loyalties all mixed up. It's easy to confuse love of a person and sweet memories of what happened in a building for love of the God whose house it is. The early Christians gathered in one cave and then another. They gathered in one person's house and then still another one. The risen Christ was with them, and they were with each other no matter where they met or with whom they met. Paul seldom stayed more than a few months as their pastor. But Christ had risen and was with them wherever they were and in whoever came forward to lead the worship.

When you move to another community, the greatest compliment you can pay your home church is to transfer immediately into another congregation of God's people.

3. Watch out for any Christian faith whose pastor and people claim a monopoly on heaven. Be careful of the pastor who claims his church is the only fold. We preachers are in a position that makes us very vulnerable to becoming ego-maniacs, jealous of each other's parishes. We can become self-centered, manipulators of people. It's always easier to persuade our people to be against something; it can become a mental illness with us. In fact, because we are sinners, it's easier to teach hate than love and acceptance.

So often all we do in church is rearrange our prejudices. Sure, it's tempting as a pastor to ignore the touchy issues like war, politics, ecology, race relations, the poor of the world, world hunger, and prison reform. One of the easiest ways to gather a large congregation and insure plenty of money for yourself and your own church is to tell people what they want to hear, to reinforce their old prejudices, to rant and rave about everyone else and thus stay off the really sensitive spot: our own shortcomings.

When a devoted old black man applied for membership in a fashionable church, the minister told him to give added consideration to his desire to join. The old man said he would go home and pray about it. When the minister saw the old black man a few days later, he asked, "What did the Lord tell you to do?" "He told me it wasn't any use," said the old man. — "He said, 'I have been trying to get in that same church for ten years and I still can't make it.' "

The more we claim exclusiveness and pour out our wrath against another denomination or race, the further we stray from the New Testament teachings and the influence of the risen Christ.

"Now, Johnny," said the teacher, "if there were 11 sheep in a field and six jumped the fence, how many would there be left?" "None," replied Johnny. "Why, yes there would," said the teacher. "No, ma'am, there wouldn't," persisted

Johnny. "You may know arithmetic, but you don't know sheep."

Sheep belong together and do just that. Johnny knew it. It's more a matter of heart and not so much of head.

All sorts of disciples saw Jesus between Easter and Ascension and in all kinds of places!

On the Emmaus Road,
in the upper room,
in the garden,
along Lake Galilee.

All sorts of persons worshiping in different ways still sense his presence. Let's try in every way possible to extend our hand in fellowship to all God's families. If there is any suspicion, let it not be from our side. We can make a grand witness of the way God would have his family join hands.

When we are baptized, we are adopted by God into a great fellowship. It's called the Communion or Fellowship of Saints. I always tell my people not to say that they have been baptized Lutherans, or Methodists, or Baptists, or Roman Catholics. I instruct them to say that they were baptized Christian and that they are now part of the Christian flock and have Christ for their Shepherd.

Many years ago, Rev. S. Parkes Cadman, in addressing a conference of ministers, said, "If you are trying to shut yourself in behind your own denominational walls, I suggest that you climb up occasionally, and look over to see how many splendid people you have shut out."

Paul says: "We are no longer strangers . . . Christ has broken down the walls that separate us."

Jesus put it: "I have other sheep who do not belong to this fold. I must lead these also, and they will hear my voice. So there will be one flock and one shepherd."

I take great heart today in the fact that:

we are baptized into God's fellowship;
beware of Christians who claim a monopoly on heaven;

*beware of basing your Christian faith on a person or a
    church rather than Christ;
don't base your religion on just what you are against;
we have one shepherd and one flock and we rejoice in the
    many folds.*

It's an old story and I have told it many times. Somewhere
out further west than we are here in Iowa, a little girl, who
had become ill, had strayed away from the farmhouse into a
large field of weeds. The mother and father had searched and
searched in the field, but could not find her. They knew if she
remained there very long in her thin nightgown, she would die
of exposure. They rang the dinner bell which signaled all the
neighbors to come in for an emergency. Farmers from all
around came to the farm and walked through the large acre-
age of weeds, criss-crossing back and forth trying to find the
little girl. It was to no avail. Then someone had a brilliant idea.
They all lined up along one fence, joined hands, and walked
through the field in an orderly fashion. About three-quarters
of the way through, one man screamed that he had found the
little girl. It was too late. She was dead. When the father got
to the scene and saw the little thing curled up in the weeds,
he exclaimed: "For God's sake, why didn't we join hands
sooner?"

Let's you and I join hands now with all of God's people.
It's a vital sign that our Lord does not still lie murdered in
a dark rock tomb halfway around the world. The fact you and
I pursue friendship and discipleship with other Christians is
a vital sign that he came out of that grave — the heart beats
— he is alive. We have a heart that produces a pulse; and the
pulse of the matter is we care and try our best to join together
with all our brothers and sisters in Christ. Amen.

The Vine And The Branches

Just outside Nazareth where Jesus grew up you can see them on both sides of the road. They grow everywhere out of that dry, rocky soil. They are the grapevines mentioned in John 15.

When I stepped off the tourist bus to take pictures, I was amazed to see these short stumps of vines lying over close to the ground and propped up with a rock to keep them off the hot red soil.

I had pictured in my mind all these years, grape arbors like grandpa's that ran from the house to the garage in the backyard and which were full of green leaves, shade, and blue grapes.

In Israel it's different. The vine is pruned back drastically. That way it has a better chance of maturing and bearing the grapes.

Jesus grew up with those vines all around his little village. He knew how you had to cut the wood to get the productive plant. He used the whole analogy as to how it is to have him as savior and belong to him.

The vine and the branches' relationship teaches us something of what our relationship to Christ is like. It teaches a Christ centrality. Whenever we forget that Christ is the heart of everything, everything goes crooked. This is true of preaching, teaching, family life, vocation — everything. Sometimes in meetings and discussions among Christians, I wish we could stop and ask, "Where does Christ fit into all of this?" Branches are grafted to the vine or they are no longer branches.

When I was a young lad on the farm in Darke County, Ohio, "Grandpa Miller," who lived across the road from us, was great for doing several things. He always helped me put rings in the nose of my pet hog, Solomi. He also was great for raising bees and rendering out the honey. But the thing that was the most fascinating about Grandpa Miller was the way he grafted apple trees. He would cut back the start of a crooked old runt tree and graft to it a fine, producing twig of a purebread tree which would mature and bring great fruit. It got its source from the strength of that stumpy tree which was cut back to the very source of life. Jesus is the very central source of our life.

One of the great evidences of the aliveness of Christ in our church and lives now is his centrality in all we do and say. The branch just can't survive without its source of life, the vine. So, too, our family of God can't be alive and survive without God being central in everything.

As we go out into the community to tell the good news to others, it must not be to feed our own ego or to get church members for our "fine church." Rather, Christ must be central; we go and witness because we love him who loves us. We go because we know the joy of being in him and want to share that privilege with others, and because we know the one who saves and wants others to know him, too.

As we serve in the church, singing in the choir, serving on a committee, working in the women's organization, we don't do it for our own gratification, but for God's. He is central; he is our vine, and from him we get our life. When we make decisions about education, where to spend our money, whom to choose as friends, what kind of lifestyle to follow, we do it with God as central. What is appropriate for one of his people is what we consider.

If God is our vine and we are his branches, then how we treat the people who live next to us becomes a religious issue. How we raise our children, how we relate to our spouse and parents are all critical issues for us who live from the vine. When God is central:

> *revenge changes to support,*
> *hate turns to love,*
> *greed moves to sharing,*
> *don't care looks like concern,*
> *and me first becomes after you.*

42

Not only that — to be a branch of the vine and have God central means:

we can relax, we have the source of life;
we can forgive, we have been forgiven;
we can share, he provides all we need;
we can care, he shows the way.

A vital sign of the alive, risen Christ of Easter is that we branches are healthy and alive, too. When it is evident we are alive and responding to the vine, then it is obvious it is an alive vine to which we are attached.

The second emphasis in our gospel is Jesus' encouraging affirmation of his disciples and us as well. Jesus and his disciples were on their way to Gethsemane. It was one of the nastiest moments of their life together. Judas had left the group in disgust; all the dreams they had dreamed about Christ's glorious future were beginning to crumble. They were nervous, edgy, and about to desert him. He affirmed them! We all need that kind of affirmation from God and from each other. Through the vine we are related to one another, and we need to support and affirm each other.

Now then, "Just how are we like the vine and the branches? Who was Jesus thinking of when he spoke of the fruitless branches?

"There are two answers to that: First, he was thinking of the Jews. They were branches of God's vine. That's the picture that prophet after prophet had drawn of them. But, they refused to listen to him; they refused to accept him; and, therefore, they were withered and useless branches.

"Second, he was thinking of something more general than that. He was thinking of Christians whose Christianity consisted of *profession* rather than *practice*, Christians whose Christianity consisted of *words* without *deeds*. He was thinking of Christians who were useless branches, all leaves and no fruit! He was also thinking of Christians who became members of the faith, who heard the message and accepted it and then fell away, who abandoned their faith, and who became traitors to the Master whom they had once pledged themselves to serve.

"So, then, there are several ways in which we can be useless branches. We can refuse to listen to Jesus Christ at all. We can listen to him, and then render him lip service unsupported by offerings or deeds. We can also accept him as Master and, then in face of the difficulties of the way or moved by the desire to do as we like and not as he likes, we can abandon him."[1]

This lesson can help us clarify some of the tension between grace and works. A branch is a branch not because of the fruit it bears, but because it belongs to the vine. If it bore no fruit, it would be a dead and useless branch. But it can't bear fruit on its own, either. It needs the nourishment, support, and growth that the roots and trunk provide.

There is something here which is imperative for us to understand. It is very risky to be one of those branches of the vine and simply not produce any fruit. In fact, if we are not fruitbearing branches, we'd better check to see into what vine we are joined! The New Testament is rather plain that if we are joined to Christ — we will produce a good fruit. If we are not producing good fruit, it probably is an indication that we aren't joined to Christ. Perhaps our vine and source of life are tradition, habit, ego, love of money, prestige, power or any of the many vines that want us for a branch.

Over and over we are asked to ". . . remain united to me (v. 4)." Paul often talks about this same idea in a mystical way. We are to be in Christ and Christ in us.

Perhaps Jesus thought of this in a much more practical fashion. He simply wanted us to know that we should keep close to him, be with others who love him, come to him often, and that way he could continue to provide us the strength and advice and love that we need to get through our days. In other words, if we want to remain the genuine grape branch we need continually to tap into the genuine grape vine.

It's just impossible to remain the good, honest, loving Christian we can be unless we continually remain close to others like that and especially to the source of all that is good and right and that's our God.

In a church building where I used to serve, we converted five Sunday school rooms into small apartments for people needing help in their lives. As long as those people lived in those apartments in the church, with all the associations of pastors and staff, they got along fine. But when they would move out into the world by themselves, they would often drift back into trouble again. They got strength and resolution for the good and decent life from its source, the Body of Christ. But when they got very far away from that source, they gave in to the ways of the world again.

An employee of the Meredith Company was walking to the parking lot after work. A train was across the walkway and a trainman encouraged her to crawl through rather than wait. Just as she started to climb over between two cars the train started up. She rode that train clear out to the edge of othe city and into the country before the train slowed enough so she could get off. She said the taxi driver laughed all the way back to town as he transported her back to the Meredith parking lot.

We can get on the wrong track like that. When we once get off our right path, we can so easily be carried away to areas of life where we really don't belong. We get further and further from that which should be our goal in life. It is in times like that we realize we have, often by accident, gone on the wrong track, and that track has carried us far from where we should be.

Our Lord knew that would be the case. He doesn't laugh at us like the cab driver; but, he does come after us and return us to where we ought to be. That is, in him, the real and true source of our lives.

It is when we remain united to him that we are then capable of producing good fruit in our lives. As long as we are far from him all the other interests of the world sap all our talents and energy. When we are united to him, then we can once more forgive, love, have sympathy, serve others, understand, and continually do the good thing. He shows us where and how and supplies the motivation and the technique.

We must keep in contact with the fine thing in order to defeat the evil and the lower thing. It's dangerous to allow ourselves to "wither on the vine" and to lose contact with Christ and his Church. Every congregation has a number on its rolls who are called "dead wood" or the inactive. These are the people who have allowed themselves to get away from the vine and get outside living in Christ.

"Being united in Christ means something like that. The vine is like a family tree. We are part of that family of God. The secret of the life of Jesus was his contact with God, his Father. Again and again, he withdrew into some solitary place to meet God.

"Jesus was always united to God. It must be so with us as we unite to Jesus. We must keep contact with him. We cannot do that unless we take definite steps to do so."[2] This is the reason for communion over and over and for regular weekly worship and for daily devotions. It's the reason the church always offers Bible study and retreats and other ways to continually deepen and strengthen our spiritual lives and our connection with the vine.

Here is a super good reason for regular worship and study. Sure, you can come to church only occasionally and still claim to be a Christian. However, there is a vine here which gives life and sustenance that we all need, and very often.

The body and blood of Jesus in the sacrament of communion are something we don't just take if communion is offered on a day we happen to come to worship. Jesus gave us this resource for life, knowing we would fall short of our discipleship, that we'd get discouraged, depressed, begin to doubt and often need that source of strength and healing forgiveness. He gave it to the disciples for that reason. We have it here for the same reason.

God knew our enthusiasm would grow weak and dissipate. He knew we'd need to hear the good news again and again from this pulpit so we might take heart again. Those who have this need have that same good news available over and over. Thus, we can be reminded, encouraged, and instructed here. It's part of being joined to the vine.

He knew we would have constant need to uphold each other, to develop deep and meaningful relationships here in his family. So he gave us this, his house, and this, his fellowship, which we might experience and enjoy. Not once when we join, but again and again. Thus, we come with the other branches to celebrate our belonging, our attachment to the vine which is God.

He knew we would need to continue to feed on him who is the source of an abundant life, that we must grow in grace all our lives. He gave us these opportunities to learn in Sunday school, in adult classes, in many ways to study and share insights about his Word.

When a medical doctor wants to check the vital signs of a body, one thing he/she checks is the pulse, that is, how is the blood flowing throughout the body. A vital sign here is if we, who are the branches, are circulating the source of life through us, and others, from the vine which is God. If Christ is out of the grave and alive with us, a vital sign will be the heartbeat; the pulse can be felt and counted and we learn, grow, expand, deepen, and continue to allow to flow throughout us, his life-giving strength and power.

Once we have been grafted to the real vine, our God, and have tasted of this spirited source of life, we'll never again be satisfied with the dry, withered life without that vine and the source. Even as the heart pumps our blood out through arteries and veins, so God wants to give from his heart life-giving strength to all of us. And, too, he wants us to be the vital sign that he is also alive and here in this place.

We have all witnessed it many times. Persons join this church and seem alive, vital, active in their spiritual lives. But, over the years, they fail to continue to grow and mature in that faith. So they "wither on the vine" and not only lose out in their own spiritual lives and possibilities, but also cause a heavy weight which drags down the entire congregation. The vine gives the life and a branch which detaches soon dries up and dies.

A vital sign of the Easter Savior alive after Good Friday is how well his disciples are attached to him, the real vine and source of life.

P. T. Forsyth wrote: "Unless there is within us that which is above us, we shall soon yield to that which is around us."

For a few of us, being united in Christ will be a mystical experience which is beyond words to express. For most of us, it will mean a constant contact with Jesus Christ. It will mean arranging life, and prayer, and worship, and silence in such a way that there is never a day when we give ourselves a chance to forget him.

Many years ago there was a convention of the Barbers Supply Association. As a publicity stunt, they went into the skid-row section of the city and found the worst drunk. He was unshaven, emaciated, and sad. They took him to a hotel, gave him a bath, a shave, a haircut, and bought him a new suit, overcoat and shoes. When he was finished, he was a marvelous example of the barbers' art. The story appeared in the press. The manager of the hotel saw it and was impressed. He told the man he would give him a job. He was to report the next day at 8 a.m. He did not appear. The manager looked for him. He went back where they found him in the first place. There he was found sleeping on some newspapers in an alley, drunk, his new clothes gone, barefooted and unshaven. Changing the outward appearance is not enough; the heart must change. We must get our sustenance from the vine which is Christ. "I am the vine, you are the branches. Those who abide in me and I in them bear much fruit, because apart from me you can do nothing (v. 5)."

Now just one warning. More drift out of the Christian life of worship and of faith than fall out. Few get angry and leave all of a sudden. But for the most part, we just drift away.

An American liner was wrecked off the Scilly Isles. The sea was calm; the weather was clear. But the ship was caught in a treacherous current which slowly, but surely, lured it out of its course.

The Associated Press carried a story that stated the following article:

"Agriculture Department scientists say a tiny parasite called a pinewood nematode poses a threat to U.S. ornamental pine trees, including Christmas tree plantings that help supplement the incomes of many farmers.

"It also is a potential threat to the nation's pine forests, says the department's Science and Education Administration. So far, in the eastern United States, the nematodes have been identified in Scotch, Austrian, White, Japanese Black, and other pine species.

"Agency scientists said they now have the methods to identify the parasite and diagnose infested wood. They hope to devise ways to control the spread of the parasite. The nematode is transmitted by beetles from infested to healthy trees."

Continually we have to be on the alert for those nematodes which will infect the branches:

> those who say don't take it so seriously,
> those who say it doesn't matter what you believe,
> those who by their example encourage a casual attitude
>   toward worship and service,
> and the more demonic ones who cause division and
>   disruption in our ranks.

Jesus advised us to remain in him, not in a preacher, a choir director, a building, a denomination, but rather, in *him*. We can easily get all confused and direct our loyalty to all sorts of people and causes and emotions rather than the one true vine.

One of the vital signs of the Easter Christ risen and alive is that his saved people remain faithful in him and he remains faithful to them.

In life, there are treacherous currents which get the soul in their grip and slowly, but surely, carry it toward the shores of ruin and wreck. Every drift ends in a wreck. When one awakens to the fact that one has been drifting, that there is not the same moral resistance, not the same eager purpose to know the truth and to do it, then it is the time to put a trumpet to the lips. It is time to live in Christ and take our proper place as a branch of the vine of Christ.

"I am the vine and you are the branches. Whoever remains in me, and I in him, will bear much fruit, for you can do nothing without me." Amen.

Easter 6
John 15:9-17

Chosen For Good News

Jesus had just told the disciples that "he is the vine and they are the branches." To disciples Jesus is speaking. The very people he chose to be with him those three years of his ministry are the ones who hear these words. While they are wondering how they got into this mess, our Lord assures them they didn't choose him, he chose them!

"I have said these things to you so that my joy may be in you, and that your joy may be complete (v. 11)."

So the disciples have the assurance that they have not chosen God, but in his grace, he approached them with a call and an offer made out of his love. It's one of the vital signs of the alive Body of Christ of Easter. He is alive and active and comes after us. Even when we don't want to be chosen, even when we hide behind our skirts of littleness and say, "Who, me?" he pursues us and continues the initiative.

If God died on that cross after saying, "It is finished," then we don't need to worry about his coming after us today and choosing us for certain privileges and responsibilities. But, if he cracked wide the tomb door and sprang out of death's grip on that first Easter, then we must consider that God is alive here, calling, gathering, sanctifying us, his disciples! It's a vital sign of the true congregation of believers.

So often we live our lives on the cross side of Easter rather than the resurrected and alive side.

What's really fascinating about this passage of Scripture is that out of it we can make a list for which we are chosen and to which we are called as God's disciples:

we are chosen for joy,
we are chosen for love,
we are chosen to be his friends.

When I was a little boy in grade school in a one-room country school in Darke County, Ohio, we used to choose up sides for softball during the lunch hour. One of the bigger boys would throw the bat in the air and another one would catch it. They would then put their fists around the bat until the man who could hold the bat with his hand last was the one that got to make the first choice. How great it was when he would choose me to be on his team. It really is a great honor and nice to be chosen. The text for today assures us who serve in the church, and especially us who are searching for a life "joy-filled," that God has chosen us. If you are hungry for a life of love and supportiveness from each other and one filled with joy, read on.

God chooses us for joy. Even when the way is very tough and trying, working toward being a full Christian becomes a joy along the way. While we struggle and worry and work, we sense a surprising joy right in the middle of all our difficulties. "I have said these things to you so that my joy may be in you and that your joy may be complete (v. 11)." There is always a sense of fulfillment and joy in doing what you are sure is right, that is good and the decent thing to do. To be dedicated toward a cause and pour yourself into it can indeed fill your life with joy of purpose.

I'll bet you've heard people say that if they miss church, they just don't feel right; or if they go there is a joy and satisfaction in going. This is often indication that here are disciples who have found rewards in serving and pouring themselves into a committed discipleship. When that element of their life is absent, they feel a great void.

Perhaps we have been misrepresenting Christ. *The Interpreter's Bible* says: "For enter a church during a time of worship, and one finds gravity and seemliness and a feeling of reverence. But would anyone, stumbling in, sense that here are people who have made a glorious discovery, and are thrilled and joy-possessed?"[1] The New Testament makes plain that those who saw Jesus in the flesh were struck almost first by a certain sunny-heartedness about him which prim minds did not easily associate with religion.

52

"The thing indeed became a scandal! 'Now John,' they said, 'with his lean, austere life in the desert, is patently a saint of God. But this other mingling in people's happiness, going to weddings and the like, is he a religious man at all?' And Jesus admitted he was happy. 'What else can we be?' he asked, 'knowing that we know, believing what we do believe, experiencing what we are experiencing day by day of the goodness of God.' . . . And indeed he was always giving thanks for something; found life a good thing . . .''[2]

A gloomy Christian is a contradiction of terms! The Christian is the person of joy; one author has called her a laughing cavalier of Christ.

It is true we are sinners, but we are redeemed sinners; therein lies joy. How can we fail to be happy when we walk the way of life with Jesus? At a church camp where I used to be director, we sang the song, "I got the joy, joy, joy, joy down in my heart." We added a verse: "And if the devil doesn't like it, he can sit on a tack, etc."

Jesus put it: "I have told you this so that my joy may be in you and that your joy may be complete."

Our Christian lives ought to reflect that joy — Jesus likened us not to a funeral procession but to a wedding reception.

Let the liturgy lift us up.
Let the hymns make a happy, easy melody.
Let the preacher smile and be enthusiastic.
Let the congregation radiate the warmth of it all.

Joy is what we are chosen for and joy is what we offer to all who come.

The earliest Christians were joyous people. The note of that first Christianity is joy. They caught the infection of that happiness from their Master. With his unsullied conscience, his uninterrupted communion with God, his perfect trust in God, his unselfish spending of himself for others, Christ must have been the happiest of men. And Christ offers to share his own fullness of joy with anyone who will accept it from him. In the Epistles and the Acts, those who have tried him keep telling us it is all gloriously true, so true it just cannot be described, we'll not go into language. Always their eyes are shining; always their hearts dance and exult in the sheer happiness of this that they have found. Clement said: "All life has become a song." Barnabas said: "Christians are the children of joy."

Paul wrote to his congregation in Philippi: ". . . I am glad and rejoice with all of you — and in the same way you also must be glad and rejoice with me (Philippians 2:17b, 18)."

Not only are we chosen for joy, but we are also chosen for love. "This is my commandment, that you love one another as I have loved you (v. 12)."

We are sent out into the world to love one another. Sometimes it doesn't look that way! Often the way we worry about our investments, the priorities we set, the time we allot to the people we're supposed to love, the way we use our resources for ourselves rather than for others, may indicate that we really weren't chosen for love.

But God has chosen us to live the kind of life that shows what is meant by loving other people.

Pygmalion labored long and carefully and produced a statue of a perfect woman. He loved the exquisite statue his genius had produced and, embracing it, kissed its cold lips. But he was loving a lifeless thing. Finally, he asked Venus, the goddess of love, to give him a living woman as beautifuil as the one he had carved. That night, when he embraced his statue, the lips were warm with life. The statue, according to the Greek myth, had become a living thing. There is mighty little life in the stranger we pass on the street or in the enemy beyond our fence; but when divine love enters our hearts, God gives to friend and foe the warmth of human fellowship.

Celsus, critic of early Christians, said: "These Christians love each other even before they are acquainted."

Jesus reminds us that he has the right to demand that of us. He says: "The greatest love a person can have for his friends is to give his life for them." And so it is that he gave his life for his friends, and you just can't have more love than that!

There are some from the pulpit and in the Sunday school room who say we should love each other — while their whole life is a demonstration of severity and revenge and an "I'll get mine" attitude.

We can be correct in our theology and yet be unkind and unloving in our practice of the Christian faith. We can practice our Christianity in a harsh and demanding way that turns people off to the love God has chosen for us.

Instead, we are to love one another. That counts under our own roof, too. Often where no one else can hear or see, where we can get by with a lot of cruelty because we are in command, we fail to practice God's love at the very place it ought to be practiced the most.

"Love one another," says Jesus. That means being sensitive to hurts and joys, to needs, to frustrations, to our spouse and children. We need to be concerned for the welfare of each other.

One little girl became angry at her mother, ran to her bedroom and locked herself in her mother's closet. The mother, being concerned about the little girl, stood by the closet door and listened. She could hear the little one gather up spit in her throat and say, "Mother, I just spit in your shoes!" Time passed. "Mother, I just spit on your new dress." Time passed. No sound. Mother finally asked, "Honey, what are you doing in there?" "I'm waiting for more spit!" That's the kind of life we can live. We can live our whole life waiting for more spit. That is, looking at ways that we might get even, get revenge, get our share, show them.

However, when we get full awareness of what love God has had for us from the cross, from the Easter resurrection, and what love he still showers upon us, not only from heaven, but from his spirit that dwells among us, then we can allow his love and our love to join forces in loving other people.

A big part of the great gospel (good news) is that we are loved by our God and by each other.

Wishing to receive the affection of his subjects, Frederick the Great struck a subject with a whip one day and exclaimed:

"Confound you! I want you to love me." We sometimes act that way. But we are chosen to love. Not forced, God takes the initiative, and chooses and comes after us.

"I love you when you're good," a father told his small daughter. The little girl answered quickly: "I love you all the time, Daddy." The little girl had the right idea of how God loves.

The grave of Charles Kingsley in Eversley churchyard is marked by a white marble cross on which are his chosen words. In Latin they mean: "We have loved, we love, we shall love."

"This is my commandment, that you love one another as I have loved you. No one has greater love than this, to lay down one's life for one's friends (vv. 12, 13)." Not only are we chosen for love, not only are we chosen for joy, — Jesus chose us to be his friends. His promise was: "I do not call you servants any longer, because the servant does not know what the master is doing; but I have called you friends, because I have made known to you everything that I have heard from my Father (v. 15)." In days gone by, to be a "servant of God" was to be one of God's elite. You were one of the great spiritual heroes of the Scripture. Moses, David, Joshua, Paul, and even James, the brother of Jesus, were proud to be God's slaves. Here, however, Jesus offers far more than servanthood. He offers friendship. With his coming into the world we have the privilege of being selected by him as his friends.

William Barclay writes in his commentary: "The idea of being a friend of God has also a background. Abraham was the friend of God (Isaiah 41:8). In Wisdom 7:27 wisdom is said to make men the friends of God. This phrase is made clear by a custom at the courts of the Roman Emperors and the Eastern Kings. A very select group who were called 'friends of the king or, the friends of the emperor' were selected. He talked to them before he talked to his generals, his rulers, his statesmen. The friends of the king were those who had the closest and the most intimate connection with him, and who had the right to come to him at any time. That's the privilege we have with God."[3]

A mother was enrolling her child in kindergarten. The teacher, following the usual procedure, began to ask questions. "Does the boy have any older brothers?" "No." "Younger brothers?" "No." "Older sisters?" "No." "Younger sisters?" "No." By this time, the lad was very self-conscious and unhappy. Defensively he said, "But, I've got friends!" And so have we.

We have a friend. A beautiful, loving friend who has worked it out for us to be God's friends. That is a super gift from our God. We don't have to see our God as way off in the sky on a cloud demanding that we do good work for him. Instead, we are close, intimate friends of his who can go right into his presence without fear.

He is no longer our slavemaster who will burn us if we don't satisfy him. We need not work like crazy to please him so he will treat us well. Instead, he comes to us as a warm and loving friend whom we then serve because that's the normal response to having a loving friend like that.

No longer fear and dread; but, rather, joy-filled friendship.

What a friend we have in Jesus,
All our sins and griefs to bear!
What a privilege to carry
Everything to God in Prayer!
                    — Joseph Scriven, 1820-86

Aristotle says among the marks of a true friend are, "He guards you when you are off your guard and does not forsake you in trouble; he even lays down his life for your sake; he restrains you from doing wrong; he enjoins you to do right . . . he reveals to you the way to heaven."

But in this succinct passage, brief though it is, Jesus Christ has given us a reading of friendship beside which the others, noble though they may be, pale like the stars when the sun rises.

For this, too, like everything else he touches, he has deepened and glorified. Real friendship between any two, he tells us, involves a certain drawing to each other, a kinship of spirit.

57

Characteristically, Christ puts first a willingness to spend one-self for the other. Aristotle had said: "Friendship seems to lie in the loving rather than in the being loved."

Also, in real friendship, there is a trust in the other that believes in him, risks on him, never doubts his loyalty, but looks toward him with confidence. It is to this intimate and whole-hearted relationship that Christ calls us today.

No longer a vengeful, much-to-be-feared God, but a warm, welcoming, accepting Father who puts his arm around us and says, "Come to me and you'll be okay." What a nice relationship Jesus worked out between us and our God!

The Interpreter's Bible says: "Buddha claimed that in his teaching he never selfishly kept a closed fist tight upon what he had discovered, but with an open hand shared everything he had learned with whoever would accept it. And, says Christ, setting it down as a proof of his friendship for us: "I have made known to you everything that I have heard from my Father (v. 15b)." And what a marvelous difference it has made that Christ was not content with thinking things out in his mind, but shared with us what he had found concerning God, and man, and life, and salvation, and a dozen other central matters. How bare and bleak and incomprehensible life would have been had he not given us his guidance, and heaped upon us discoveries which we could not have made."[4]

It's a tremendous thing that Christ, in spite of all our failings and false starts, still considers us his friends and trusts us like one friend trusts another. Amazing as it seems, we who are the little people of this world have been hoisted up to the high place to be God's friends. It's his choice.

These, then, are the three things we disciples are called for — they are a magnificent challenge and promise to us today:

> *chosen to be his friends,*
> *chosen for love,*
> *chosen for joy.*

I have told you this so that my joy may be in you and that your joy may be complete. My commandment is this: love one another, just as I love you . . . I do not call you servants any longer, . . . I call you friends.''

"Are you medical or surgical?" asked one small boy of another in the hospital ward. "I don't know," replied the youngster. The questioner was scornful, having been a patient in the hospital for some monoths. Condescendingly, he undertook to make his meaning plainer for the sake of the other lad: "Were you sick when you came in, or did they make you sick after you got here?" he inquired.

Sometimes it seems as though we get more gloomy after we get here! But a vital sign of an alive Body of Christ here is friends, love and joy — it's the pulse of any alive God present.

Friends of God, let's you and me love one another and share his joy. Amen.

A Prayer For Disciples

If we want to know what is most important in someone's heart, we ought to hear what they pray and what they say as they know they are facing death. All the other incidentals and trivia are stripped away and we speak our deepest concern, our most avid and desperate worry at a time like that. It is for that reason this prayer of Jesus recorded in John 17 is of such importance:

"Holy Father, protect them in your name that you have given me, so that they may be one, as we are one (v. 11b)."

Jesus knew he now faced the cross in Jerusalem. He was speaking to God about great and serious concerns he had before his death. And what were those important concerns?"

> *That those who followed him might not misunderstand and try to withdraw from the world.*
> *That his disciples would remain united and one.*
> *That God would protect his disciples from evil.*
> *That his disciples be equipped with a heart and mind which would enable them to meet the challenge of discipleship.*

Let's look, then, at these items that hung so heavy on our Master's heart and see what they mean for us in this church and in this day.

Jesus prayed that his disciples would remain in the world. "I am not asking you to take them out of the world, but I ask you to protect them from the evil one (v. 15)."

It's easy to think we should escape from the world and its temptations when we take on discipleship. Our Lord had a different idea! He saw discipleship as equipment to get through

61

but never the means to avoid the trip. So, he called his disciples to a life of activity and service rather than retreat and seclusion. Not into the monastery but out into the world. Not out of, but into. That was his prayer and that is our directive.

Remember how Peter, James, and John had such a tremendous experience on the Mount of Transfiguration? God appeared to them in a cloud, spoke to Jesus, and Jesus even had a change in his appearance to the disciples. It was such a nice religious and emotional experience that Peter wanted to build a church and stay there. But Jesus informed him that disciples, after having a religious experience, must go down into the valley, into the world, and serve other people. That's the kind of discipleship Jesus was praying for those disciples.

Of course, there is a very important place in our life for worship and for prayer; we need always to study and deepen our spiritual lives. But, discipleship means action; it means to live and serve in the world around us.

"Don't coop your soul in a corner," urged St. Theresa of the young women she was training.

Jesus died for our forgiveness in order that we might be put right again with our God. When that happens, we must go out into the world to minister with an enthusiasm for sharing all the undeserved we have received. There are those who are hungry and thirsty; there are those who are cold and shunned; there are those who don't know the joy of belonging to God's family like we do. All are waiting. It's just not correct or even recommended that we retreat to a withdrawn spiritual life. Out into the world, that's where the disciple's action is.

"As Lord Rosebery, the British Prime Minister, wrote of the purposeful and striking saintliness of the great Thomas Chalmers: 'Again, it should be said that his saintliness was not that of an anchorite brooding in religious solitude. Here was a man, bustling, striving, organizing, speaking and preaching with the dust and fire of the world on his clothes, but carrying his shrine with him everywhere.' "[1]

There is a rhythm in discipleship life — into the presence of God, out into the world. William Barclay puts it: "Of course, there is need for quiet times, times when we shut the door upon the world to be alone with God, but all these things are not the end of life; they are the means to the end; and the end of life is to demonstrate the Christian life in the ordinary work of the world."

We can easily violate Jesus' prayer for us here! We often see our Christianity as a release from our problems — rather than a way to work through them to a solution. Troubles are not escaped or evaded here, they are faced and conquered![2]

So, if you are hurting plenty:

with a disastrous marriage,
or a son or daughter is a problem,
or money is a terrible worry,
or you lost your job,
or a friend disappointed you,

God offers here, not escape from those problems, but the equipment to face them squarely and, with his help, to not only survive, but to do it with victory.

Jesus knew that one of the vital signs of an alive Christ after his crucifixion and resurrection would be response. That is, there would need to be a response from the Body of Christ for help to those who need, definite, practical help for life and all its complexities. Then others who saw the church would know that Christ really lives in them because through them they are helped. There is direct help when people have needs. That's a vital sign that he is alive still and now.

In order to provide that help for all who need, disciples had to be available in the world. Their religion had to talk about earthly matters and gut issues. Their worship language needed to be understandable and their worship practices meaningful. Everyday problems like marriage relations, trouble with children, sex, morals, ethical decisions all needed to be addressed.

It was, and still is, vital that the Body of Christ be the alive instrument through which Jesus' prayer for us is answered. Here in the world, on the cutting edge of life, we practice his alive presence.

Jesus prayed it for us: "I do not ask you to take them out of the world, but I do ask you to keep them safe . . ." Rather than finding ways to abandon this world, we will always try to win it, assured he will keep us safe.

Jesus also prayed for our unity: "Keep them safe by the power of your name, the name you gave me, so that they may be one just as you and I are one."

As Jesus prayed this prayer for the 12 disciples — it was a bold prayer — they would be against insurmountable odds. Yet, said Christ, they can do it because it's you and me and them and they can win the victory.

Jesus knew that when the disciples quarreled, picked at each other, allowed jealousies, bickered, continued to complain, the cause of his Christianity was severely damaged. So he prayed for unity.

That doesn't mean we all have to agree or think alike. It doesn't mean we all have to have the same opinions. But, it does mean there is one great, overriding principle we all are motivated by and will stand for and work toward. On this we are totally united. The gospel of salvation — the presence of Jesus the Christ — must be shared here. It is his church, his love, his forgiveness, his service to others we are and do.

As the ages come and go, Jesus says there are a couple of the supreme requirements of his church. First, that we should deepen our relationship to God, allow him to come to us and be always very near. And, out of that flows the second, that we will then become very close to each other. It is often true that because we live too far from God that we remain so distant from each other.

The gospel of Jesus Christ — that is, the good news about our God, that he loves us and forgives us and takes us into his family — that gospel cannot truly be preached and effectively experienced unless we are one united family of brothers and sisters.

We must also say it here: Competing churches, jealously in congregations and between congregations, exclusiveness and divisions, do continually tear down that which is very precious to our Savior. Jesus prayed that we, his disciples, might be united just like he and his Father were united.

Jesus prayed that we might have God's protection against evil. ". . . I do ask you to keep them safe from the evil one (v. 15b)."

I cannot explain where the evil comes from or just exactly why it is present. I do know that there is a strong power that works against God; and that power is subtle, and smart, and clever, and attractive. Call that power demon, devil, evil one, or Satan, or just plain us.

I did read once of a lawyer who went to a judge to complain that the client for whom he had just won a case had refused to pay his fee. "Did you present your request in writing?" asked the judge. "Yes, I did, sir," replied the lawyer. "And what did he have to say?" continued the judge. "He told me to go to the devil," answered the lawyer. "Then what did you do?" "Well, then I came straight to you, sir."

No matter what you name it, we all know it continually presents a real danger to us.

There is a story that Alexander the Great once sent to a certain province a beautiful maiden whose breath was like perfume of the richest flowers. All of her life, however, she had lived amid poison, inhaling it until her body was full of poison. Flowers presented to her withered on her breath, and if she breathed on a bird, it fell dead. The legend embodies the truth that there are lives in whose presence nothing pure or beautiful can thrive, and whose moral breath is corruption and death.[3]

Not a man with horns and pitchfork and red underwear and with a tail, but a power that has dressed up and joined the church and that makes evil very tempting and respectable. Jesus knew that and prayed God to keep us safe from that evil which tempts us on every side.

"A man once dreamed he was in Hell. When asked to give an account of what he had seen — if there were flames there, and suffering there, and wrecked and maligned creatures with whom he had to associate — he said, 'Yes, but there was something far worse than that; I was compelled to face my influence. I knew that I deserved punishment, for I had scorned and rejected Jesus Christ; but my sorest pain was to see what the effect of my life had been upon others.' "[4]

It's a great thing to remember when we are tempted to be destructive and mean and ungodly, that God himself is standing over our lives, trying to guard us and keep us safe. Especially when we try to live our lives on our own strength and cleverness this evil power is effective. It is then we must remember Jesus worked it out for his disciples to remain safe amidst all the evil of this world — with his presence and support protecting us.

". . . I do ask you to keep them safe from the evil one." Jesus prays his disciples might have a heart and mind of truth which would enable them to carry out their discipleship. "Sanctify them in the truth; your word is truth (v. 17)."

The word translated dedicate here means "to set apart for a special task." Indeed our Lord's prayer for us wants us to be set apart for a special holy task.

There are a number of examples in the Old Testament when God called and his people were set apart for a very special job:

> *Jeremiah 1:4 — Now the word of the Lord came to me saying, "Before I formed you in the womb I knew you, and before you were born I consecrated you; I appointed you a prophet to the nations."*
>
> *Exodus 28:41 — You shall put them on your brother Aaron, and on his sons with him, and shall anoint them and ordain them and consecrate them, so that they may serve me as priests.*
>
> *Exodus 3:10 — Moses stood at the burning bush and God gave to him a very specific responsibility to carry out. "So come, I will send you to Pharaoh to bring my people, the Israelites, out of Egypt."*

But the words to dedicate can also mean to equip a person with the qualities of mind and heart and character which are important for the job to be done. If those disciples were to be effective servants of Christ — their lives had to look and to be Christ-like — they must ring true.

"When workers in marble in ancient Rome accidentally chipped their statues, they would fill in the chipped places with wax of the same color as the marble and then sell their work as perfectly wrought. Other statue makers, wishing to sell honest products, stamped their product *sine cera* (without wax). From this custom has come the modern word "sincere."[6] Jesus prayed his disciples might be sincere.

That's so true for us. If we are to serve a holy God, we must live holy lives. So God not only selects us to be his disciples, but he also equips us with the qualities of life to carry out the task we have been given. In other words, God selects us to be his disciples, but he doesn't let it go at that; he continues to equip and help us with that which he has chosen us to do.

Jesus is praying here: "Help them to devote themselves to it without reservation and as the end and purpose of their lives. Accept them as a people dedicated to your service, to the spreading of the truth, and the sharing with others what I have brought to them from you."

He wanted them to catch the inspiration of his spirit, so that they might be utterly unable to keep out of this adventure, but would have to throw themselves into it. Given those elements, he felt anything and everything was possible.

That's our Lord's prayer for his disciples and for us. He was really saying in effect, "Once you have selected them, God, for this holy and sacred task, stick with them and enable them to do it in truth and sincerity. Help them so they are not only set apart to be disciples, but are also given your presence and help through the whole of the discipleship that they must do."

This means when God, through another member, the pastor, a committee, asks us to be true to our calling of discipleship, and to do a job for them, we do it in a special fashion. When we're asked to help with the feeding, clothing, comforting, exhorting, standing for justice, contributing, helping to do the witnessing, he goes with us and helps us as we try to do our best. "Dedicate them to yourself by means of the truth; your Word is truth. I sent them into the world, just as you sent me into the world (v. 18)."

It's a great discipleship to which the out-of-the-grave and alive Master calls us. But just because he did come out of that grave, he can call us to such an exciting mission and service. He prayed for those early disciples and for us, that we would be set apart, equipped to carry out our discipleship, kept safe by him from all evil, united in a common cause and family, and out in the thick of things doing our discipleship.

It is a vital sign of the Body's life: The way and amount of discipleship we carry out as a result of our lives in him and he in us. And how great it is that he has prayed we might have God's help as we carry it out here.

It's a beautiful prayer: "I do not ask you to take them out of the world, keep them one just as you and I are one, keep them safe from the evil one, and dedicate them to yourself by means of the truth." Amen.

Ascension Of Our Lord
Luke 24:44-53

The Friendly Skies — United

It simply was unthinkable that the appearances of Jesus should grow fewer and fewer after Easter until they finally "petered out" and melted away. That would have effectively weakened the faith of all people who had seen him. There had to come a day of dividing — when Jesus of earth became Christ of heaven.

The Ascension must always remain a mystery to us, for it attempts to put into words what is beyond words and to describe what is beyond description. Something like this had to happen. It was just essential. One way God had related to us had to stop and a new way had to begin.

Luke tells it this way: "Then he led them out as far as Bethany, and lifting up his hands, he blessed them. While he was blessing them, he withdrew from them and was carried up into heaven. And they worshiped him, and returned to Jerusalem with great joy; and they were continually in the temple blessing God (vv.50-53)."

It had been 40 days for the disciples, 40 extraordinary days! Jesus was crucified; Calvary was an ugly experience. He came out of the grave on Easter and came to them in the upper room where they had cowered together hiding from the Temple authorities. Then, 40 days of fishing and talking and eating and just being together. Now he was going to leave; — the Scripture puts it: "When he had said this, as they were watching, he was lifted up, and a cloud took him out of their sight (Acts 1:9)."

Until this day, the skies were not friendly. The Old Testament told of a God who wanted to punish and get even. People lived in terror of the Creator. Jesus told of one who is love and who was so concerned for their guilt and shame he would

69

give his Son on the cross. So they came to this hill outside Jerusalem and it was there that he ascended.

The battle had been won against sin and death. The great example of what God is like had been lived out in Palestine. A ministry had been done around Galilee. So he ascended; the Scripture says up. That is not important; what is important is that he returned to make it possible to now be with us.

We can be sure the skies above are (like United Airlines calls them) friendly skies now. That is — we have a Savior who worked out a way to be our advocate and helper, to be with us now. No longer need we feel alone, or ever afraid. The skies are friendly. He is there and here. And that's the nice thing about God. After Jesus came out of the grave and was again alive and with the disciples, the whole thing just couldn't peter out. And so there was a definite end to this method of being with his people and a start of a new way of existence, — a new presence of God in our lives. The Jesus of earth becomes the Christ of heaven.

On this Ascension Eve, let's look at what the Ascension meant to the disciples.

It was an ending. One stage was passed and another had begun. The day when their faith was faith in a flesh and blood person, and when it depended on the presence of that person's flesh and blood, was ended. Now they were linked to someone who was forever independent of space and time.

It's the same with us. It would be hard for us if Christ had not ascended. Now we have the spirit as well as the Christians in Jerusalem. Now we don't have to travel halfway around the world and back 2,000 years to find God with us. This makes him more than a Bible hero! It also moves him from long ago and far away to here and now.

The plan of Emmanuel of Christmas is complete. God is indeed with us and here. So we see the end of one way God related to human beings whom he had created, and the brand new beginning of another way.

A while ago, I heard a pastor tell of burying the son of a father and mother who had become estranged and divorced and now lived in separate cities. It was a very difficult funeral. The pastor claimed that he selected his words carefully at the funeral home. The father and mother rode in separate cars to the cemetery. After the committal service and genuine expression of a lot of grief, the pastor walked away from the grave back to the funeral coach. He turned to see the father and mother holding hands at the graveside. He returned to the graveside and they spoke these words: "It took the death of our son to bring us together again."

God saw that it was going to be necessary to come in human flesh, be a son, and die on the cross in order to rejoin us with him. He had accomplished that in the person of Jesus Christ. Now that time had come to an end and that plan had been worked out and completed. All the possibilities are now there that because of the death of his Son, you and I can have forgiveness and be rejoined with him and belong to his family.

This was also, and equally, a beginning as well as an ending. The disciples did not leave the scene heartbroken; they left with great joy . . . "they returned to Jerusalem with great joy." They left that way because now they knew that they had a Master from whom nothing could separate them anymore.

I know not where his islands lift
Their fronded palms in air;
I only know I cannot drift
Beyond his love and care.

In *A Treasury of Sermon Illustrations,* J. C. Mitchell writes: "Anton Reicha, the great conductor, was rehearsing his choir for a production of *The Messiah.* The choruses had sung through to the point where the soprano takes up the refrain, 'I know that my Redeemer liveth.' The technique of the soloist was perfect — faultless breathing, accurate note placing, splendid enunciation. When the final note died away, all eyes turned to Reicha for his approval. Instead he walked up to the singer with sorrowful eyes and said quietly: 'My daughter, you do not know that your Redeemer lives, do you?' She flushed and replied, 'Why, yes, I think I do.' 'Then sing it,' cried the conductor. 'Sing it so that all who hear you may know that you know the joy and power of it.' And he motioned the orchestra to play again. When the singer finished this time, the old master approached, saying, 'You do know, for you have told me.' "[1]

We need to live out our lives in worship and service in such a way that it is obvious we are convinced a new relationship to us has been begun by God. Sometimes it doesn't look like it in the way we worship.

Mark Twain used to tell the story of a person who had been in prison for five years. When they finally unlocked the door so that he could walk out, he remained for two more days without noticing. That's just the point. God has given us a new relationship to him which ought to free us up so that we live our lives, order our priorities, and relate to other people in a different way.

"For I am convinced that neither death, nor life, nor angels, nor rulers, nor things present, nor things to come, nor powers, nor height, nor depth, nor anything else in all creation, will be able to separate us from the love of God in Christ Jesus our Lord (Romans 8:38-39)."

That's important to us, isn't it? No military, no ruler, no husband, wife, or sister or daughter, no thing of being or pressure can take him from us now. Everything else is very temporary. We can lose it all, but not our relationship with God. He has worked it out to be with us here and to see us through whatever we must face.

Christians can rejoice that God has ended the time when he was Jesus of Nazareth in Palestine so that he might go to the cross and come out of the grave. Christians can rejoice even more that God has begun a new way to be with us after this Ascension. He is here and close to us and gives us the support and strength and encouragement necessary for each day that we live.

One of the vital signs of a live Christ, out of the grave, up to heaven, and back with us here, is his presence now. A sure sign he did come out of that grave and is alive is the present help he gives us here. If we are worshiping a dead martyr, that's one thing. But, if he is alive, a vital sign which proves this to us is the help he is to us now:

When a loved one dies;
When our children disappoint us;
When a spouse is found unfaithful;
When friends hurt us;
When it just doesn't seem like it's worth going on any longer.

The skies can be friendly. God does want to comfort and give peace. Solace and encouragement are available.

Paul found him an ever-present help. Martin Luther sensed profound encouragement from him. Kathryn Koob, that deeply spiritual hostage in Iran, knew his support during her 444 days of captivity. All the great spiritual heroes of the past haven't been such perfect people; but, rather, they have known the friendly skies — that magnificent, loving, strong, support of the ever-present, risen Christ.

It's a great vital sign, our risen Christ helping here and now.

Still further, the Ascension gave the disciples the certainty that they had a friend, not only on earth, but also in heaven.

I find great comfort in this fact. For those who have lost loved ones, for those who grieve over people very dear to them, there is a definite promise that in heaven there awaits us that selfsame Jesus who on earth was so kind and so sensitive and so concerned.

To die is not to go out into the dark alone, but it is to go to him. He reminded his disciples shortly before this in John 14:2 . . . "In my Father's house there are many dwelling places, . . . I go to prepare a place for you." This Ascension night he is on his way to the united skies to make them friendly for us when we must also dwell there.

I think we could say it is correct to claim that most do not regard heaven as some local place beyond the sky. We regard heaven as a state of blessedness when we will be forever and inseparably with God. It is this heaven that God is preparing on this Day of Ascension.

When I had a student pilot's license and then got permission to haul passengers as I flew a small Cessna airplane, I took my six-year-old son up above 7,000 feet. It was always a magnificent experience to fly through the clouds and go up on top where the sun was shining. I'll never forget the first time he saw that beautiful heaven. He looked puzzled for a minute and then asked, "Where's the angels and the harps?" We now know that heaven is more a state of being than it is a place. Nevertheless, the Ascension was a visible thing that God acted out through Jesus so that those who 2,000 years ago believed in a flat earth with a place called heaven just beyond would be confident that God dwells there and was ready to care for them at the time of their death. Wherever heaven is, and however it is, you can bet your life and death on this fact: It's going to be friendly and a place has already been selected for us.

If Jesus was to give his followers unanswerable proof that he had returned to his spiritual state, the Ascension was just absolutely necessary. If we carefully read the description of the Scripture, we do not need to think in terms of a countdown and a launch like a Gemini rocket. Rather, we can see a changing into a spiritual relationship instead of a local and physical one on that mountaintop outside the city of Jerusalem.

Notice that the Scripture tells us that the disciples went back to the temple in Jerusalem praising God. Luke's gospel began there in the temple with Elizabeth and Zacharias. Now it ends in the same temple, a full witness of what had come out of those believing members of that holy place.

To have a friend in heaven and to know the skies are friendly is a magnificent fact of assurance while we live out the reminder of our physical life here.

"How do you know your mother is upstairs?" inquired a man of his nephews who were studying their church school lesson. "The Ascension. I saw her go," answered one of them.

74

"You mean you saw her start upstairs," said the uncle. "Perhaps she did not get there and she may not be there now even if she has been there." "I know she is there," said the youngest child, "because I went to the foot of the stairs and called her and she answered me."

The disciples said they saw their Master ascend into heaven, and they knew he was living. That is not as strong a proof as that he speaks to me and I know it is his voice. It is a friendly voice. Yes, Christ rose from the dead and ascended into heaven. We believe it on the testimony of the gospels. But we believe it especially because we hear the voice and see the works of the living, reigning Christ here. We feel his real presence in this fellowship.

United Airlines calls for us to "Fly the Friendly Skies, United." That is another element in this ascension story: These disciples were united. Because of what they had witnessed, they could now unite for one common purpose.

It ought to be that way for us disciples, too. It ought to be one of the vital signs of the Christ alive body. United Christians working together, and worshiping one Christ, is a potent vital sign that he is alive.

What other cause could unite such a diverse people as we? Who else could hold together such sinners from such varied backgrounds as ours? Only an alive, risen Christ. We, as we work and worship, study and serve, make a great witness (a vital sign) to all who see us that he is alive.

When we come to a full realization that we, of all people, have Almighty God here with us, that that same God gave his Son on a cross for our sins, that he came out of the grave, that he worked it out to come here and be with us, that makes us different.

Our priorities change. Our church membership changes. Our marriages change. Our friends change. Our very life changes. The skies are no longer unfriendly. Nor are we any longer unfriendly.

Differences in race and sex and origin melt away. Contempt for the poor and unfortunate leaves. Hostilities disappear. The skies are friendly and because of that — *so are we.*

Those things which seemed hopeless take on hope.
Those circumstances that drag us down now look
  different.
We can love the unlovely.
We can celebrate when everyone else wants to mourn.
We can manage depression and inflation and depletion
  and competition.
Our lives are lived under friendly skies with an alive God
  present.

We give thanks tonight that Jesus is no longer one person in one city. As we extinguish the paschal candle which represented his physical presence on earth after coming out of the tomb until tonight, we also light other candles in our hearts because he is here now. We rejoice that our risen Savior is a spirit that is among us and especially with us as we worship together.

To help all of us who are weak and not sure, he gives us:

this fellowship and experience,
this joy which we feel,
this equipment to face and live life now.

So we see the Ascension was an ending — one stage had passed and another had begun. It was a beginning; a new spiritual relationship with God is now possible. And it gives us a certainty we have a friend in heaven.

There's no doubt about it, we celebrate tonight the fact that the skies are again friendly. And we are united.

It says at the end of this Ascension story: "And they worshiped him, and returned to Jerusalem with great joy; and they were continually in the temple blessing God (Luke 24:52-53)."

Let that be a description of us tonight. Amen.

Notes

When Thomas Doubted
1. William Barclay, *The Gospel of John,* Vol. 2, *The Daily Bible Series.* (Philadelphia: The Westminster Press, 1955), p. 321.
2. *The Interpreter's Bible,* Vol. 8 (Copyright renewal © 1980 by Abingdon. Used by permission.)
3. *op. cit.,* pp. 321 and 322.
4. John Rilling, *Insights,* JLJ Publishers, Springfield, Ohio.
5. *Ibid.*
6. William Barclay, *op. cit.* p. 322.
7. *Ibid.,* p. 323.

The Vine And The Branches
1. William Barclay, *The Gospel of John,* vol. 2, *The Daily Study Bible Series.* (Philadelphia: The Westminster Press, 1950), p. 204.
2. *Ibid.*

Chosen For Good News
1, *The Interpreter's Bible,* Vol. 8 (Nashville: Abingdon-Cokesbury Press, 1952), p. 722.
2. *Ibid.* p. 722.
3. William Barclay, *The Gospel of John,* Vol. 2, *The Daily Study Bible Series.* (Philadelphia: The Westminster Press, 1955), p. 208.
4. *The Interpreter's Bible, op. cit.,* 724.

A Prayer For Disciples
1. *The Interpreter's Bible,* Vol. 8 (Nashville: Abingdon-Cokesbury Press, 1952), p. 750.
2. William Barclay, *The Gospel of John,* Vol. 2, *The Daily Study Bible Series,* (Philadelphia: The Westminster Press, 1955), p. 252.

3. Clarence E. McCartney, *McCartney's Illustrations* (New York: Abingdon Press), p. 188.
4. *Ibid.,* p. 187.
5. William Barclay, *op. cit.,* p. 253.
6. *A Treasury of Sermon Illustrations,* ed., Charles L. Wallis (Nashville: Abingdon-Cokesbury Press, 1950), No. 2335, p. 280.

The Friendly Skies — United

1. *A Treasury of Sermon Illustrations,* ed. Charles L. Wallis (Nashville: Abingdon-Cokesbury Press, 1950), No. 334, p. 50.